USING THIS BOOK

One of the best ways of helping children to read, is by reading stories to them and with them.

If you have been reading earlier books in this series, you will be used to reading the story from the left-hand pages only, with words and sentences under the illustrations for the children to read.

In this book, the story is printed on both the left and right-hand pages.

The first time you read the book, read the whole story, both left and right-hand pages, aloud to the child and look at the illustrations together.

When the book is next read, you read the text on the left-hand page and the child, in turn, reads the text on the right-hand page, and so on, through the book.

British Library Cataloguing in Publication Data
McCullagh, Sheila K.
    The Silver River. — (Puddle Lane. Stage 4; v. 5)
    1. Readers — 1950-
    I. Title   II. Davis, Jon   III. Series
    428.6   PZ7
    ISBN 0-7214-0970-9

First edition

Published by Ladybird Books Ltd Loughborough Leicestershire UK
Ladybird Books Inc Lewiston Maine 04240 USA

ⓒ Text and layout SHEILA McCULLAGH MCMLXXXVI
ⓒ In publication LADYBIRD BOOKS LTD MCMLXXXVI

The
Silver River

written by SHEILA McCULLAGH
illustrated by JON DAVIS

This book belongs to:

Ladybird Books

The story so far:

The iron boy and the sandalwood girl
were going to the Blue Mountains,
in the magical Country of Zorn.
They were looking for the Silver River,
because the Magician had told them
that if they washed in the Silver River
they would become truly alive,
like other children.
In the Country of Zorn,
they met three silver ponies,
who had wings, and could fly.
One of the ponies took the iron boy
and the sandalwood girl on his back.

The three silver ponies
ran along the bank
of the river.
They opened their wings,
and flew up into the sky.

As the sun came up, the iron boy
and the sandalwood girl could see
the Country of Zorn below them.
And all the time, ahead of them,
they could see the Blue Mountains,
with their tops covered in snow.
As they came to the mountains,
the two other ponies left them
and flew away, along a wide valley.
But the pony carrying the iron boy
and the sandalwood girl
flew higher and higher,
into the mountains, until
they had nearly reached the snow.

They could see great rocks
below them.
There were deep valleys
in the mountains.

At last, they saw a great ridge
of rock.
There was a wide round hole
in the ridge, which looked as if
it had been cut out of the mountain.
There was an arch at one side,
where the mountain top rose up
towards the sky.

A river ran out of the arch,
and fell down into the hole
in a great white waterfall.

The silver pony flew out over
the great hole. He circled round,
so that they could look down.
"That's the river, the Silver River,"
he cried, as he flew through
the spray from the waterfall.
Far below them, they saw the river
splashing down into a great pool.
On the far side of the pool,
there was a big cave.

The river ran into the cave,
and on, under the mountain.

The pony landed on the edge
of the cliff.
"You must go on yourselves, now,"
he said. "I must fly home."

"But how can we reach the river?"
asked the sandalwood girl.

"There's a path down the cliff
on this side," said the pony.
The sandalwood girl and
the iron boy crept to the edge
of the cliff, and looked down.
The cliff was very high and steep,
and the water was far below them.
They could see a narrow path
leading down, but it looked
very dangerous.

They went back to the pony.
"Is there any other way?"
asked the iron boy.

"There is no other way,"
said the pony.

"We might climb down that path",
said the sandalwood girl. "But
we could never climb up again."

"You won't need to climb up,"
said the silver pony. "The river
flows into the cave. The cave
runs right under the mountain
to the Great Valley of Zorn,
where the people of Zorn live.
I have never been there myself,
but I have met the people of Zorn
in the mountains.
Once you get to the Valley of Zorn,
the people of Zorn will look after you.
Goodbye, iron boy.
Goodbye, sandalwood girl."

The silver pony opened his wings,
and flew away,
back down the mountain.

The iron boy and the sandalwood girl
went back to the edge of the cliff, and
looked down at the path.
They both felt frightened.
''We must go,'' said the iron boy.
''There's no other way, if we want
to wash in the Silver River,
and become truly alive,
like other children.''
They began to climb down.
Before very long, it was so steep
and so narrow, that it wasn't
really a path at all.

The iron boy and
the sandalwood girl
climbed slowly down,
holding on to the rock.

Because they were made of wood and
iron, they moved slowly and stiffly.
The rock was slippery, and
they held on to it with their hands
where they could.
The iron boy tried to kick footholds
with his iron feet, but the rock
was very hard.
But they climbed on, down and
down and down.
They tried not to look at the
water, far below them.

Then the iron boy's foot
slipped on the hard rock,
and he almost fell.
But the sandalwood girl
pulled him back to the path.

They stood still for a moment,
holding on to the rock.
They felt almost too frightened
to move.
But after a few minutes,
they began climbing down again.
''I can see a rock below us,
jutting out over the water,''
said the iron boy.
''If we climb down there,
we can rest.''
The sandalwood girl looked down.

But as she looked,
the rock she was holding
came away in her hand.

The iron boy caught her dress,
and pulled her back against the rock.
She managed to find a place
for her feet, but
she was very frightened.
The iron boy could feel her shaking.
They stood still again
for a few minutes, and then
they began to climb down
once more, until at last
they reached the rock, which
jutted out over the water,
like a shelf.

But there was no way down
from the rock.
''It's the end of the path,''
said the iron boy.

He looked at the cliff.
It was like a steep wall,
and they were still high
above the water.
"We can't climb down there,"
he said.

"Look!" said the sandalwood girl.
She pointed over the water.
"Look at the big cave.
The pony was right.
There's a path there,
into the mountain."
From where they stood,
they could see into the big cave.
Silver moss was growing
on the walls.

There were steps cut in the rock,
and there was a path,
along by the river.

"Do you think the Magician was right?"
said the iron boy.
"Suppose he was wrong?
Then I should sink down
to the bottom of the river, and
that would be the end of me."

"We shall have to trust him,"
said the sandalwood girl.
"We can't climb back up the cliff.
If you are still made of iron
when we fall in the water,
I shall still be made of wood.
I'll try to hold you up,
as I did before,
when the bridge broke, and
we fell into the river."

The iron boy looked up at the cliff.
"We'll go," he said. "We can't climb
back. We'll trust the Magician."

They stood on the rock,
hand in hand.
"Jump!" cried the iron boy.
And they jumped down,
into the Silver River.

They fell down, under the water.
But as they plunged into the Silver River,
a great change came over them.
The iron boy suddenly found
that he wasn't sinking to the bottom.
He kicked his legs, and came up
to the surface. He could swim!
And the sandalwood girl
didn't float on the water.
She went under, too, and
she had to swim. But
her legs weren't stiff any more
and she moved her arms easily!

"We've changed!" cried
the sandalwood girl.
"We're truly alive!
We're real children!"

They swam across to the cave,
and climbed up the steps
to the path.
"We've changed!"
cried the sandalwood girl again.
"The Magician was right!
We changed, in the Silver River."

"The cave seems much smaller,"
said the iron boy.

"It's not the cave, it's us,"
said the sandalwood girl.
"The cave isn't smaller.
We're bigger.
We're real children now."

The iron boy and
the sandalwood girl
were so happy that
they began to dance.

They jumped into the air,
and they shouted.
They held hands and twisted
round and round.
They forgot that they were tired.
They forgot that they didn't know
where they were going.
They danced and danced,
and jumped about, and shouted,
until at last they were out of breath.
"We're alive!"
cried the sandalwood girl.
"We're really and truly alive!"
They could scarcely believe it.

"I'm hungry," said the iron boy.
"You don't feel hungry,
when you are made of iron.
But you do when you are alive."

"I'm hungry, too,"
said the sandalwood girl.
"Let's go along the path, and see
if we can find the great valley
the silver pony told us about."
They turned along the path,
into the cave.
It wasn't dark, because the silver moss
on the walls was shining brightly.
The river ran along beside the path.

They had not gone far,
when they saw a light
coming towards them.

A tall woman carrying a lantern
was coming along the path.
She wore a long white tunic,
and a cloak.
"Who are you?" she asked
in a kindly voice.
"And where have you come from?"

"We have come down the cliff,"
said the iron boy.
"I was made of iron,
but when I jumped into the Silver River,
I wasn't iron any longer."

"And I was made of sandalwood,"
said the girl.
"We both came to the Blue Mountains,
to find the Silver River.
When we jumped in, we changed.
We're alive now. We're truly alive."

"But we don't know our names,"
said the iron boy.
"The Magician said I should find
a name, when I found the river."

"A boy made of iron, and
a girl, made of sandalwood!"
exclaimed the woman.
"I know your names."
She turned to the iron boy.
"Your name is Irun," she said.
She turned to the sandalwood girl.
"You are called Sandella, and my name
is Alanna, and I come from
the Valley of Zorn."

"How do you know our names?"
asked Irun.

"Because there is a story
in the Valley of Zorn," said Alanna.
"I have heard it since I was a child.
It is about an iron boy and
a sandalwood girl, who will come
over the mountains one day.
Their names are Irun and Sandella,
and the story says that
they will live in the Country of Zorn,
and do many wonderful things,
as they grow up.
You must be Irun and Sandella.
I'm glad you have come at last."

Then Alanna gave Irun and Sandella
some little cakes to eat,
and they didn't feel tired
any more.

Sandella and Irun walked on
through the cave with Alanna,
until they came to the other end,
and saw the Great Valley of Zorn
spread out before them.
Not far away, they could see
the towers of a big city.
"You can live there, in my home,"
said Alanna.

So Irun and Sandella went with
Alanna to the wonderful city of Zorn.

Notes for the parent/teacher

In the stories in the books at Stage 4, the child is asked to read part of the main story and not just the sentences under illustrations. This is a big step forward.

If you read the whole of the story to the child first, it will make the reading much easier for him or her. But some children still need the chance to read quietly to themselves the pages that they will later read aloud with you.

Reading a story aloud on sight, without having had a chance to look at the text first, is one of the most advanced and difficult kinds of reading. If when the child is reading aloud, he/she reads the words in such a way that the story makes sense but the words are not exactly the same as those in the book, don't correct this on a first reading. This shows that the child understands the meaning even though he/she gives that meaning in his/her own words. On later readings, you should ask the child to look carefully at what was there in the book. The illustrations will give lots of helpful clues.

Remember always that both you and your child should **enjoy** your reading sessions. Keep the book, even when the child can read his/her part of it easily and has gone on to other, more difficult books. Children will later reach a stage when they can read the whole story for themselves.